Spent the afternoon @
the park with the kids.
Came home dirty & happy.
Luv having built-in playmates.
#FatherhoodPerks

Father & son moment:
Spring training =
Spring fever =
We r believers.
#SportyDad

For:
From:
Date:

Compiled by Kathryn Deering in association with Snapdragon Group℠, Tulsa, OK.
Text talk by Jonathan Lutherbeck.

ISBN 978-1-61626-614-1



Published by Barbour Publishing, Inc., P.O. Box 719, Uhrichsville, Ohio 44683,
www.barbourbooks.com

*Our mission is to publish and distribute inspirational products offering exceptional value and biblical encouragement to the masses.*

Printed in China.

# A Little Book of tweets

for

Dads

Innovation King @ his best: put ankle weights on the legs of the umbrella stroller 2 keep it from tipping over. We dads r paragons of simple solutions.

#DaddioSays: "@Kiddos, u have the right 2 remain silent. Right now that's probably the best option 4 u. Where's ur mother?"

Dad's take on hospitality:
"Tact is the art of making guests feel @ home when that's really where u wish they were."
—Abraham Lincoln

Snow has been a real problem 4 my golf game. Guzzling 2 much clubhouse coffee. #SportyDad

Teaching the youngest
how 2 take out the trash
is waaaay more work
than just doing it myself.
#WhoseKidsRThese?

Dear God, thnk U 4 blessing me with kids. Pls b my guide as I try 2 raise them in a way that honors U above all else. Amen.

"Baseball is 90 percent mental, the other half is physical."

—Yogi Berra

I think u could say the same thing about fatherhood some days!

Looking @ family vaca pics from last yr. Boy, we have some fun times 2gether! #FatherhoodPerks

Business trips r fun,
but my favorite thing about
them is coming home 2 big
hugs & lots of kisses from the
wife & kids. #LuvMyLife

"Hope is a verb with
its shirt sleeves rolled up."
—David Orr

Advice 2 dads:
Trust ur child-rearing
instincts, cherish ur spouse,
& enjoy every moment.

I used 2 think Disney
movies were boring.
Now that I've had 2 watch
4,275 of them (multiple times),
I'm starting 2 see the appeal.

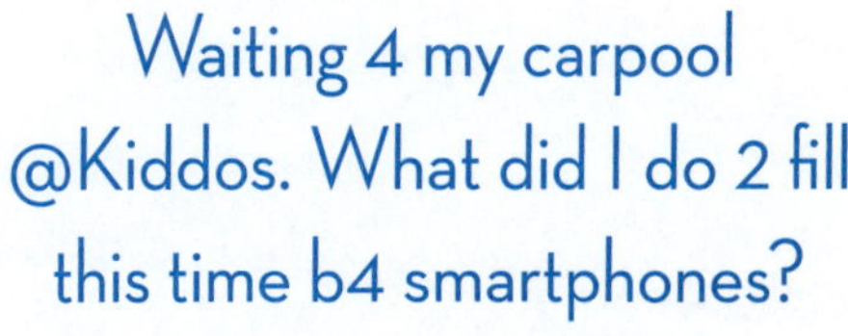

Waiting 4 my carpool @Kiddos. What did I do 2 fill this time b4 smartphones?

*Sniff, Sniff*

"When u have brought up kids, there r memories u store directly in ur tear ducts."

—Robert Brault

Repaired the garbage disposal. Found a Spiderman (minus a right arm) in the hopper. Nobody's confessed 2 the crime yet. #WhoseKidsRThese?

@Kiddos asked me y my hot dogs taste so good. #DaddioSays it's bcuz he's king of the grill! #FatherhoodPerks

I've already had a workout 2day since "Laughter is inner jogging" (Norman Cousins). My kids make me LOL every day!

My baby grl has me wrapped tightly around her little finger. It hurts so good. #LuvMyLife

Never met a basket of wings I didn't like. Neither have my kids—I barely get any! #TheyTakeAfterDad

"Spring is nature's way of saying 'Let's party!'" (Robin Williams). The grill's heating up. Come on over!

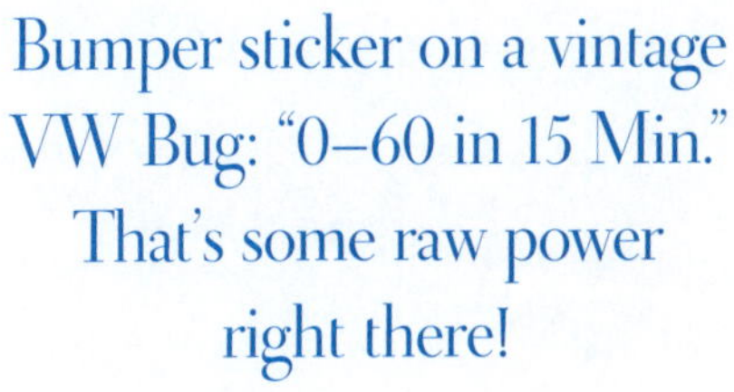

Bumper sticker on a vintage VW Bug: "0–60 in 15 Min." That's some raw power right there!

Statistically proven:
Put a pic of ur kid in ur wallet.
If u ever lose ur wallet,
u r more likely 2 get it back.

@Wifey, u do such a great job with the @Kiddos. Thnk u 4 making being their dad such a joy. #LuvMyLife

@Kiddo #2 asked 2 try my coffee this morning. He said he didn't like it & asked y I drink it. "So I can keep up with u," I replied.

Washed the car with
the @Kiddos.
AKA taught them how 2
spray each other with the hose.
#TheyTakeAfterDad

@Kiddos r growing up 2 fast.
"Time is an illusion."
—Douglas Adams

Coaching a preschool soccer team is like herding cats. #WhoseKidsRThese?

Best moment of my day:
Walking thru the door @ the
end of the day 2 hear excited
shouts of "Dad's home!"
#LuvMyLife

Having these little faces around, watching my every move, depending on me, makes me appreciate my dad more every day. Luv u, Dad.

"2day is the oldest u've ever been, yet the youngest u'll ever b. Enjoy this day while it lasts."

—Unknown

Dads need grace 2:
"Just bcuz nobody
complains doesn't mean
all parachutes r perfect."
—Benny Hill

RIP, old beat-up laptop. U were a martyr 4 the family cause. Thnks 4 the games, e-mails, family pics, & keeping the @Kiddos occupied.

God, sometimes I look @ my
family & I get overwhelmed
with the responsibility of it all.
But U r always with me,
no matter what. Thnk U.

Family truism:
"Sometimes the difficulty in choosing teams isn't having an odd number of ppl. It's having a number of odd ppl."
—Steve Clark

18 holes of golf. 4 lost balls.
1 wet ball. A day outside
on the course with the kids
cheering me on, priceless.
#LuvMyLife

#DaddioSays:
"My @Wifey's always complaining I don't take her anyplace expensive. But hey, I just took her 2 the gas station."

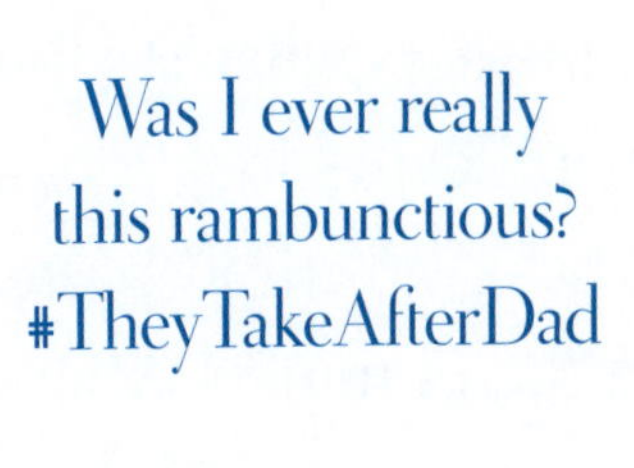

Was I ever really
this rambunctious?
#TheyTakeAfterDad

Some days when it's loud around here I look forward 2 being an empty nester. But then I think, "Who will I roughhouse with?"

My daughter's sporting events r overlapping with my son's. Can I simulcast myself? #SportyDad

Not all dads r hapless sitcom guys. "I not only use all the brains that I have, but all that I can borrow."

—Woodrow Wilson

Wisdom from Dad:
"U can't overestimate the unimportance of practically everything."

Christmas morning is more fun with kids bcuz of 1 word: TOYS! #TheyTakeAfterDad

Played tea party with the little grls. I like tea & cookies. Wasn't keen on the tutu dress code (but I played along). #WhoseKidsRThese?

Another reason it's great
2 b a dad: adding lacrosse
2 my coaching résumé.
#FatherhoodPerks

#DaddioSays: "U know u r a dad if u would give ur right arm 2 b ambidextrous."

Afternoon fun: Folding paper airplanes & flying them in the backyard. The kids' r better than mine. #TheyTakeAfterDad

This guy must b talking about me: "If u can count ur $, u don't have a billion dollars."

—J. Paul Getty

"Families r like fudge. . .
mostly sweet with
a few nuts."

—Unknown

Observations from the family car: No, we aren't there yet. & we probably won't b there yet the next time u ask, either.

Monopoly with the family. More like cut-throat big business. My competitive genes run deep. #TheyTakeAfterDad

Guilty as charged: "Children r natural mimics who act like their parents, despite every effort 2 teach them good manners."

—Unknown

Like Dan Quayle,
"I deserve respect 4 the
things I did not do."

What happens between the time a @Kiddo is 2 young but begs 2 mow the yard & the time he's old enuf but hides when the grass is long?

I'm getting the pruning shears:
"A man's children & his garden
both reflect the amount of
weeding done during the
growing season."
—Unknown

Saturday family project:
Bathe the pets. Lots of
suds & giggling. We made
new memories & marginally
cleaner animals.

Luv our pets, but when it comes down 2 it: "My favorite animal is steak."

—Fran Lebowitz

"There is only 1 way 2
bring up a child in the way
he should go, & that is 2
travel that way urself."

—Abraham Lincoln

Shopping with @Wifey & teenage daughter—my own version of the economic stimulus plan.

#DaddioSays: "1 day I woke up & realized I was old. B4 that I felt like I was only about 25."

"The happiest moments of my life have been the few which I have passed @ home in the bosom of my family."

—Thomas Jefferson

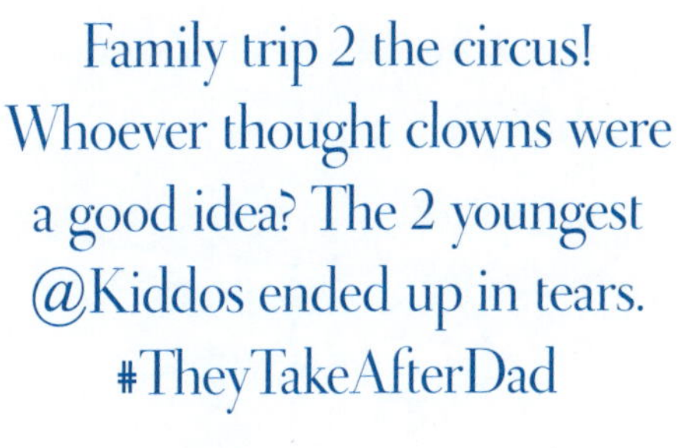

Family trip 2 the circus! Whoever thought clowns were a good idea? The 2 youngest @Kiddos ended up in tears. #TheyTakeAfterDad

"If u want children 2 keep their feet on the ground, put some responsibility on their shoulders."

—Abigail Van Buren

Haven't been fishing in yrs,
since BC (b4 children).
It's quiet out here without the
@Kiddos. I should b relaxed,
but instead I'm unnerved.

Learned the hard way as a dad: "Things which matter most must never b @ the mercy of things which matter least."

—Goethe

My @Kiddos respond 2 my advice the same way I responded 2 my dad: complete indifference. When they have kids they will understand.

Held the door open 4 @Wifey, & my @Kiddo says, "How primitive, Dad." Then he just walked on thru the open door himself. #WhoseKidsRThese?

@No.1Daughter posted the following—I must b doing something right: "Smoothies with my hero AKA my best friend & father. I luv u, Dad."

Found a note from the
youngest @Kiddo in my
briefcase 2day: "Dad,
I miss u when u r @ work.
Come home soon. I luv u."
#LuvMyLife

True @ wrk, true @ play:
"Ability will never catch up
with the demand 4 it."
—Malcolm Forbes

@DaddioSays: "When I see the ripped-up yard where the slip 'n' slide was used all day, I remind myself we're raising @Kiddos, not grass."

@Wifey had the @Kiddos put Valentine cards in my lunch box 2day. Best lunch ever. #FatherhoodPerks

This guy definitely should've stopped 2 ask 4 directions: "I don't even know what street Canada is on."

—Al Capone

Now that minivans r cool
again, I can finally hang
my head high (right?).
#FatherhoodPerks

@Kiddos & I made dinner
2night 2 give @Wifey a break.
It was fun making such a mess.
Not so fun cleaning it up.
#TheyTakeAfterDad

Heigh-ho, Silver!

"An intellectual snob is some1 who can listen 2 the William Tell Overture & not think of The Lone Ranger."

—Dan Rather

I am a bad patient when I get sick. Poor @Wifey has another (big) kid 2 take care of! Note 2 self: order flowers.

Camping in the backyard with @Kiddos this weekend. Time 2 bust out my s'mores secret: peanut butter cups instead of chocolate bars! Shh!

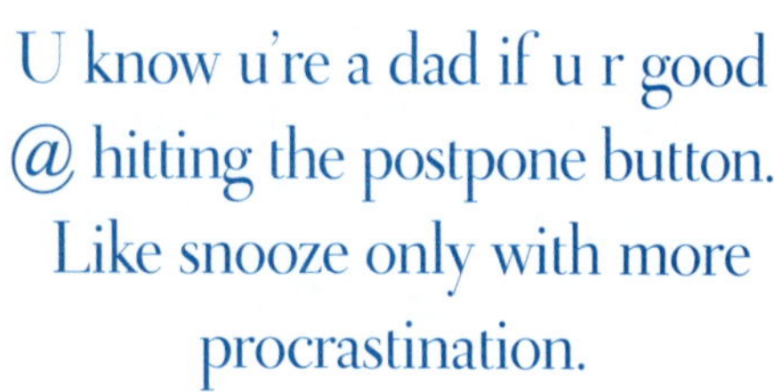

U know u're a dad if u r good @ hitting the postpone button. Like snooze only with more procrastination.

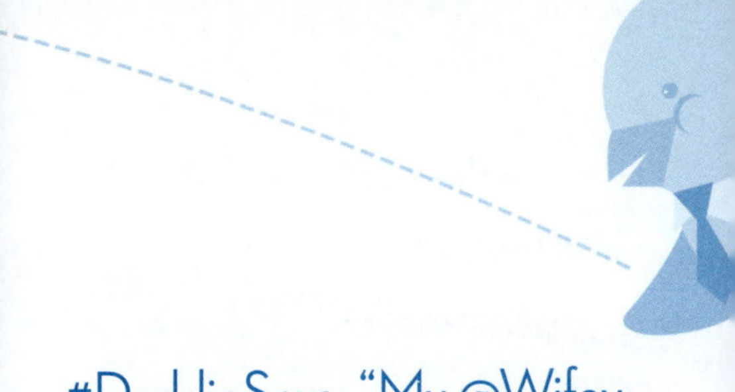

#DaddioSays: "My @Wifey is always late. Her ancestors arrived on the Juneflower."

Rough night: "Last night I dreamed I ate a 10-pound marshmallow, & when I woke up, the pillow was gone."

—Tommy Cooper

So far, 2 out of 3 @Kiddos have needed braces. & #3 is shaping up 2 make it a perfect batting average. Good-bye, $.

Give peace a chance:
"What can u do 2 promote
world peace? Go home
& luv ur family."
—Mother Teresa

Fatherly observation:
The rainy days I save
4 usually seem 2 arrive
during my vaca.

@Wifey keeps threatening 2 record me when I'm sleeping. "Laugh & the world laughs with u, snore & u sleep alone."

—Anthony Burgess

I'm sure I looked awkward holding my @Kiddos 4 the first time. Tiny babies feel weird in a dad's big hands! Glad I got used 2 it quickly.

Friday evening go-carting with the family! They ate my dust! Pretty sure I could race NASCAR if I found a sponsor. #SportyDad

Is there anything more American than a dad taking his @Kiddos 2 a Saturday afternoon baseball game? Go team! #LuvMyLife

I luv driving the @Kiddos nuts by listening 2 oldies. Someday they will appreciate the greatness. #WhoseKidsRThese?

Good advice, especially 4 dads:
"If u wouldn't write it & sign it,
don't say it."
—Earl Wilson

@No.1Daughter: Dad, can we watch something else?
Me: This game is only on once a yr. @No.1Daughter: U can watch it next yr then.

If a catnap is a short snooze,
then a dadnap should b a 3-hour
afternoon hibernation.
I need a dadnap right about now.

Amen, bro! "B4 I got married, I had 6 theories about bringing up children. Now I have 6 children & no theories."

—John Wilmot

#DaddioSays: "Any man can b a father. It takes some1 special 2 b a daddy."

Dear God, I never understood how hard it was 4 U 2 let Ur Son leave Ur side 2 come 2 earth. Now that I'm a dad, I get it. Thnk U.

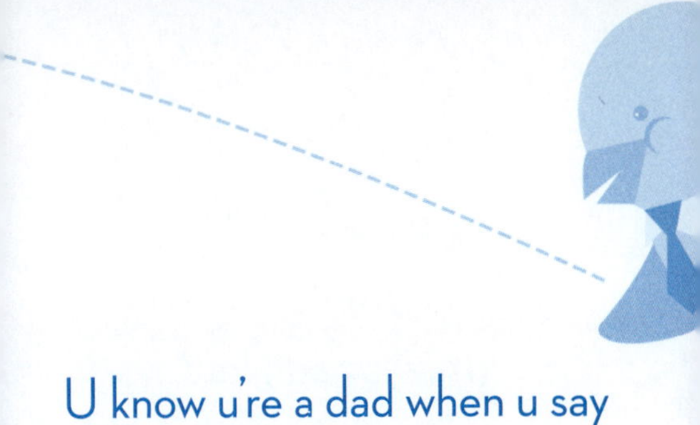

U know u're a dad when u say things like, "Don't ask me, ask ur mother!"

"Here is a test 2 find out whether ur mission in life is complete. If u're alive, it isn't."

—Richard Bach

#DaddioSays: "I don't mind parent-teacher conferences much. I just find the tiny desks & chairs 2 b really uncomfortable."

I'm taking notes from this guy:
"If u command wisely, u'll b
obeyed cheerfully."
—Thomas Fuller

Found my childhood Red Ryder wagon in my parents' garage. Cleaned it up with a coat of paint & it's ready 4 new memories with my @Kiddos.

"Every time I see an adult on a bicycle, I no longer despair 4 the future of the human race."

—H. G. Wells

Every member of the family has a bike now. Look out world, here we come! (Fasten ur helmet!) #LuvMyLife

"There r 3 stages in a [dad's] life—nutrition, dentition, & tuition."

—Marcelene Cox

Sending the @Kiddos
2 summer camp 2day.
@Wifey & I will enjoy
a day or 2 of quiet,
then we'll b ready 2
have their chaos back.

#DaddioSays:
"Rap is 2 music what
Etch A Sketch is 2 art."

U know u're a dad when u say things like, "We're not lost. I'm just not sure where we r."

Ignorance is bliss: "Ur children tell u casually yrs later what it would have killed u with worry 2 know @ the time."

—Mignon McLaughlin

Nice try, NPR,
but interrupting ur own
stories 2 ask me 4 $ is
already my 13-yr-old's thing.

@Kiddo #3 never stops talking. Ever. Mom told me I'd have a kid just like me someday. Here he is! #TheyTakeAfterDad

"It takes a strong sense of humor 2 b a father."

—Conover Swofford

I'm not sure the logic holds here: "U should always go 2 other ppl's funerals; otherwise, they won't come 2 urs."

—Yogi Berra

Road trip! "If all the cars in the U.S. were placed end 2 end, it would probably b Labor Day weekend."

—Doug Larson

"It's never 2 late 2 have a happy childhood."
—Berke Breathed

I want this bumper sticker:
Dyslexics of the World, Untie!

@Kiddo is a born comedian. @Kiddo: What do u call a grizzly with no teeth? Me: What? @Kiddo: A gummy bear!

#DaddioSays: "I wondered what it'd b like when my @Kiddos got 2 the age where everything I do embarrasses them. Secretly, I enjoy it."

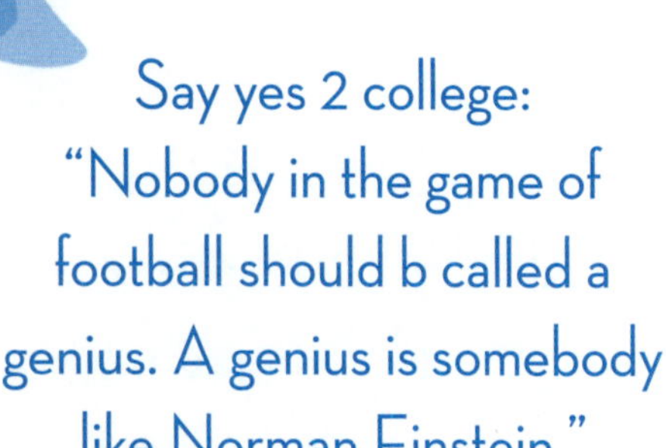

Say yes 2 college:
"Nobody in the game of football should b called a genius. A genius is somebody like Norman Einstein."
—Joe Theismann

Advice from old Dad:
"Go the extra mile.
It's never crowded."
—Unknown

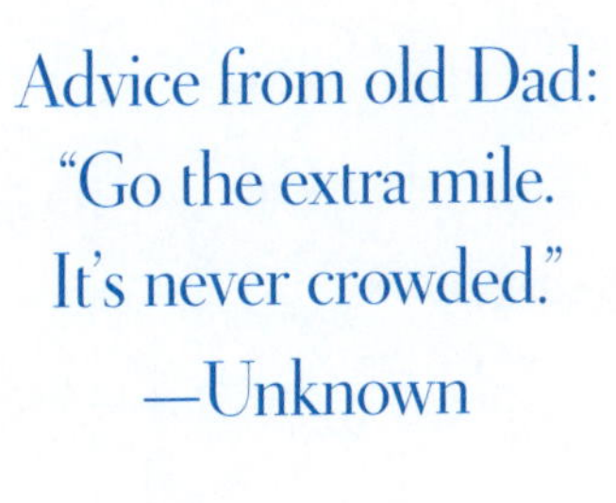

"Every child comes with the message that God is not yet discouraged of man."

—Rabindranath Tagore

I think there's no better way 2 stay young than regularly playing with the @Kiddos. Except 4 the next morning's aches & pains. #SportyDad

"Experience is that marvelous thing that enables u 2 recognize a mistake when u make it again."

— Franklin P. Jones

Dad confession: "It's really hard 4 me 2 let my @Kiddos beat me @ anything. @ least their video gaming skills keep me humble."

@Wifey asked me 2 fix my 3-yr-old daughter's hair this morning. Major Dad fail. Somehow they both still luv me.

Dad @ mealtimes = plate cleaner 4 the @Kiddos. My waistline is reaping the benefits. . .not in a good way! #FatherhoodPerks

"The surest sign that intelligent life exists elsewhere in the universe is that none of it has tried 2 contact us."

—Bill Watterson

@Wifey is a born multitasker. When I try, I just manage 2 screw up several things @ once. We make a great team!

Us dads gots smarts: "Beauty is the wisdom of women. Wisdom is the beauty of men."

—Chinese Proverb

"Human beings r the only creatures that allow their children 2 come back home."

—Bill Cosby

#DaddioSays:

"The minivan is a gas hog. Segways 4 every1!"

I'm going grayer by the min.
"Children r a great comfort
in ur old age—& they help
u reach it faster, 2."
—Lionel Kauffman

U know u're a dad when u say things like, "In my day. . ."

@Kiddos r covering their ears: "There's no half singing in the shower. U're either a rock star or an opera diva."

—Josh Groban

I'm sorry if u've had 2 fly with my family: "In America there r 2 classes of travel—first class, & with children."

—Robert Benchley

Reminded my @Kiddos of this truth 2day: "4 every min u r angry, u lose 60 seconds of happiness."

—Unknown

This dad could learn a thing or 2 from this guy: "Drawing on my fine command of the English language, I said nothing."

—Robert Benchley

#DaddioSays: "The single activity almost guaranteed 2 raise ur blood pressure & shorten ur life is teaching ur firstborn 2 drive."

God, disciplining my @Kiddos isn't my favorite thing 2 do, but I know it's necessary bcuz I luv them. U probably feel the same about me.

"Give a person a fish & u feed them 4 a day; teach that person 2 use the Internet & they won't bother u 4 weeks."

—Dave Barry

I'm banking on this 2 b true:
"Sometimes the poorest man leaves his children the richest inheritance."
—Ruth E. Renkel